Heroes and Villains

Guided/Group Reading Notes

Brown Band

Contents

OXFORD

Introduction

Reading progression in Year 3/Primary 4

In Year 3/P4 (ages 7–8) the majority of children have mastered the basics of learning to read and the focus is on continuing to build their engagement with reading, supporting their reading confidence, further developing comprehension and increasing reading fluency. Phonic knowledge still plays a role in decoding some new words and in spelling but the majority of everyday words are now recognized automatically. Year 3/P4 children can read longer texts with less explicit support from repeated vocabulary and sentences and from pictures. Familiar and regular words, now part of children's sight vocabulary, are used to provide a secure reading base. New vocabulary is increasingly varied and includes polysyllabic and more complex topic-based words. Introducing new vocabulary within meaningful context is an important element in extending children's vocabulary range.

The texts at **brown band** contain a variety of sentence structures, vocabulary and verb tenses. Children will encounter complex, fast-moving plots which engage interest and encourage the reader to read on through a whole book. The plot is developed over several chapters. Events are extended over a longer period of time. Some events may be told in a 'non-chronological' order through time-slip or flashback devices. Insights into characters' motives, feelings and actions become increasingly complex and characters are presented through a range of means: thoughts, feelings, behaviour, actions and responses to other characters. The consequences of actions are explored and moral dilemmas posed. Literary language is core and clearly distinct from the everyday language of character dialogue. Language play (puns, homonyms, jokes, onomatopoeia, etc.) can also be found in the texts. Stories are not merely straightforward recounts but demand inference, deduction and synthesizing of information from the reader.

In non-fiction books, the content of the text is largely outside of the reader's direct everyday experience – thus broadening their knowledge and their vocabulary. Texts have depth and lots of opportunity for the reader to infer, interpret and evaluate information – the text poses questions to the reader and/or encourages them to investigate a subject further. The ratio of text to illustrations/photographs is greater, but the illustrations continue to provide additional information and interest for the reader, including opportunities to compare and contrast visual information and source materials.

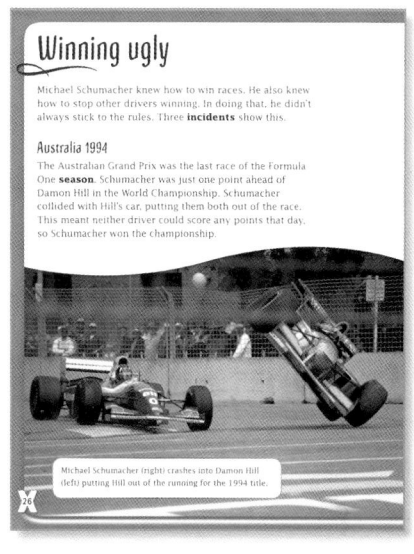

A range of non-fiction features including charts, maps, tables, labelled diagrams, captions, indexes and glossaries are used to encourage children to read and interpret information presented in a variety of ways.

Visual literacy is supported through additional action and information in the illustrations, the use of graphic devices and cartoon and comic-strip genres and the suggestions for visualization comprehension strategies suggested in these notes.

Progression in the Project X character books

In this cluster, the children are introduced to a new character, Dani Day, a Junior Scientist, who innocently goes to work for Dr X at NASTI headquarters. Dani, however, quickly sees through his evil ruse and sides with the children, knowing that they are in danger because they possess the watches which Dr X continues to pursue. In *Heroine in Hiding*, Dani escapes in a flying X-Pod to warn the children of the danger they are in and tries to convince them – unsuccessfully – to give her the watches.

Guided/group reading

The engaging content and careful levelling of Project X books makes them ideal for use in guided/group reading sessions. The advantages of using guided/group reading, as well as charts to help you assess the appropriate level for a reading group, are discussed in the *Teaching Handbook* for Year 3/P4.

To use the books in guided/group reading sessions, you should select a book at a band that creates a small degree of challenge for the group of pupils. Typically, children should be able to read about 90% of the book unaided. This level of 'readability' provides the context for children to practise their reading and build reading confidence. The 'challenge' in the text provides opportunities for explicitly teaching reading skills.

These *Guided/Group Reading Notes* provide support for each book in the cluster, along with suggestions for follow-up activities. Each book can be covered in up to three guided/group reading sessions. Alternatively, children may read much of each book independently and only undertake one guided/group reading session around the text. Although guided/group reading suggestions for all of the book are given under each section of the notes, teachers will select which chapters/non-fiction spreads they wish to use in guided/group reading sessions.

Speaking, listening and drama

Talk is crucial to learning. Children need plenty of opportunities to express their ideas through talk and drama, and to listen to and watch the ideas of others. These processes are important for building reading engagement, personal response and understanding. Suggestions for speaking, listening and drama are given for every book.

Within these *Guided/Group Reading Notes* the speaking and listening activities are linked to the reading assessment focuses.

Building comprehension

Understanding what we have read is at the heart of reading. To help readers become effective in comprehending a text these *Guided/Group Reading Notes* contain practical strategies to develop the following important aspects of comprehension:

- Previewing
- Predicting
- Activating and building prior knowledge
- Questioning
- Recalling
- Visualizing and other sensory responses
- Deducting, inferring and drawing conclusions
- Determining importance
- Synthesizing
- Empathizing
- Summarizing
- Personal response, including adopting a critical stance

The research basis and rationale for focusing on these aspects of comprehension is given in the *Teaching Handbook* for Year 3/P4.

Reading fluency

Reading fluency combines automatic word recognition, reading with pace, and expression. Rereading, fluency and building comprehension are linked together in a complex interrelationship, where each supports the other. This is discussed more fully in the *Teaching Handbook* for Year 3/P4. Opportunities for children to read aloud are important in building fluency and reading aloud to children provides models of expressive fluent reading. Suggestions for purposeful and enjoyable oral reading and rereading/re-listening activities are given in the follow-up activities to guided/group reading and in the notes for parents on the inside cover of each book.

The Project X *Interactive Stories* software can be used to provide a model of reading fluency for the whole class and/or opportunities for individuals or small groups of children to listen to stories again and again. Listening to stories being read is particularly effective with EAL children. The titles *Air Scare* and *Heroine in Hiding* are included on the CD-ROM for Year 3/P4.

Building vocabulary

Explicit work on enriching vocabulary is important in building reading fluency and comprehension. Repeatedly encountering a word and its variants helps it become known on sight. The thematic 'cluster' structure of Project X supports this because words are repeated within and across the books. Suggestions for vocabulary work are included in these notes. The vocabulary chart on pages 10 and 11 shows when vocabulary is repeated and new words are introduced. It also indicates those words that can be used to support learning alongside a structured phonics and spelling programme.

Developing a thematic approach

Helping children make links in their learning supports their development as learners. All the books in this cluster focus on the theme, **Heroes and Villains**. A chart showing the cross-curricular potential of this theme is given in the *Teaching Handbook* for Year 3/P4, along with a rationale for using thematic approaches. Some suggestions for cross-curricular activities are also given in these notes, in the follow-up suggestions for each book.

In guided/group reading sessions, you will also want to encourage children to make links between the books in the cluster. Grouping books in a cluster allows readers to make links between characters, events and actions across the books. This enables readers to build a complex understanding of characters gradually, to give reasons why things happen and how characters may change and develop. It can help them recognize cause and effect. It helps children reflect on the skill of determining importance, as a minor incident or detail in one book may prove to have greater significance when considered across several books.

Note that the books in this cluster can be read in any order.

In the **Heroes and Villains** cluster, some of the suggested links that can be explored include:

- making model aeroplanes with features such as ailerons, rudders and propellers. (**Art and design**)
- holding a mock trial to present two sides of a character from history. (**History**)
- making shoe box models of NICE and NASTI headquarters and using them to create an animation of the story using small world people. (**DT**)
- discussing moral issues such as distorting the truth, talking about people behind their backs and being fair. (**PSHE**)

Reading into writing

The Project X books provide both models and inspiration to support children's writing. Brief suggestions for relevant, contextualized and interesting writing activities are given in the follow-up activities for each book. These include both short and longer writing opportunities. The activities cover a wide range of writing contexts so writers can develop an understanding of adapting their writing for different audiences and purposes.

The Project X *Interactive Stories* software contains a collection of 'clip art' assets from the characters books – characters, setting and props – that children can use in their writing.

There are also a number of writing frames that can be printed for children to use, or that children can write/type into directly to practise writing and ICT skills.

Selecting follow-up activities

These *Guided/Group Reading Notes* give many ideas for follow-up activities. Some of these can be completed within the reading session. Some are longer activities that will need to be worked on over time. You should select those activities that are most appropriate for your pupils. It is not expected that you would complete all the suggested activities.

Home/school reading

Books used in a guided/group reading session can also be used in home/school reading programmes.

Before a guided/group reading session, the child could:
- read the first chapter/chapters and the guided/group reading session begin at the next unread chapter
- read a related book from the cluster to build background knowledge.

Following a guided/group reading session, the child could:
- reread the book at home to build reading confidence and fluency
- read the next chapter in a longer book
- read a related book from the cluster.

Advice for parents on supporting their child in reading at home is provided in the inside covers of individual books. There is further advice for teachers concerning home/school reading partnerships in the *Teaching Handbook* for Year 3/P4.

Assessment

During guided/group reading, teachers make ongoing assessments of individuals and of the group. Reading targets are indicated for each book and you should assess against these reading targets. You should select just one or two targets at a time as the focus for the group. The same target can be appropriate for several literacy sessions or over several texts.

Readers should be encouraged to self-assess and peer-assess against the target/s.

Further support for assessing pupils' progress is provided in the *Teaching Handbook* for Year 2/P3.

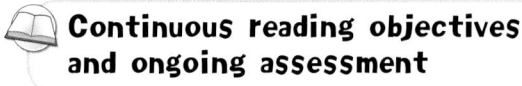

Continuous reading objectives and ongoing assessment

The following objectives will continue to be consolidated in guided/group reading sessions in Year 3/P4. Teachers will be aware of these objectives in their ongoing assessment but will only specifically assess against these objectives for children who are not making the expected rate of progress:

- Read independently and with increasing fluency longer and less familiar texts **5.1**
- Know how to tackle unfamiliar words that are not completely decodable **5.3**
- Read and spell less common alternative graphemes including trigraphs **5.4**
- Read high and medium frequency words independently and automatically **5.5**

The following objective will be supported in every guided reading session and is therefore a continuous focus for attention and assessment (AF1). This objective is not repeated in full in each set of notes but as you listen to individual children reading you should undertake ongoing assessment against this objective as children encounter new words in their reading:

- Use syntax, context and word structure to build their store of vocabulary as they read for meaning **7.4**

Further objectives are provided as a focus within the notes for each book. Correlation to the specific objectives/guidelines within Scottish, Welsh and Northern Ireland curricula are provided in the *Teaching Handbook* for Year 3/P4.

 ## Recording assessment

The assessment chart for the **Heroes and Villains** cluster is provided in the *Teaching Handbook* for Year 3/P4.

 ## Diagnostic assessment

If an individual child is failing to make good progress or he or she seems to have a specific problem with some aspect of reading you will want to undertake a more detailed assessment. Details of how to use running records for diagnostic assessment are given in the *Teaching Handbook* for Year 3/P4.

Vocabulary chart

At Year 3/P4, the children should:

- read high and medium frequency words independently and automatically
- read and spell
  - compound words and polysyllabic words
  - prefixes and suffixes
  - unfamiliar words using known conventions.

NB Examples only are given in each category.

Air Scare	Phonetically regular compound and polysyllabic words	take-off, backwards, competition, competitors, judge, engine, helicopter, vertical
	Prefixes/suffixes	-ing carrying, gathering, sticking, causing, blowing, buzzing, nothing, gleaming, roaring, steering, speeding, clapping, streaming, satisfying, responding, jostling, struggling
	Context vocabulary	fuselage, rudder, ailerons, cockpit, remote control, streamlined, wingspan, launch, propeller, biplane, battery, terminal, joystick, manual control
Heroine in Hiding	Phonetically regular compound and polysyllabic words	computer, invention, perfect, password, collection, silver, dangerous, straight, holographic, cupboard, corridor, navigation, underground
	Prefixes/suffixes	-ly actually, clearly, exactly, lonely
	Context vocabulary	heroine, nano technology, astronomy, physics, biochemistry, intelligence, scientist, science, laboratory, machine, dial, launch, robots, micro, engine

Dr X's Top 10 Villains	Phonetically regular compound and polysyllabic words	powerful, despicable, mastermind, superhuman, complicated, criminal, broadcast
	Prefixes/suffixes	**-tion** animation, inventions, competition, science fiction, domination, protection, ambitions **-ic** robotic, scientific, magnetic
	Context vocabulary	console, technology, mutant, nuclear, clones, engineer, mechanical, intelligent, genius, laboratory, cyborg, implants, revenge, enemy, exterminate, experiment
Jake Jones v Vlad the Bad	Phonetically regular compound and polysyllabic words	secret, overlords, signal, motorbike, zookeeper, chitchat, museum, curator, vanilla, vegetable, velociraptor, Viking, vowels, verbs, volleyball, volcano, vulture, vulcanized, Violet, vinegar, Viennese, vase, vervet, Venus, Valentine, Vesuvius, video, villainous
	Prefixes/suffixes	**-ed** one-eyed, waxed, rumoured, flashed, demanded, flipped, vanished, switched, scanned, vulcanized, remembered, defeated, sprinted
	Context vocabulary	SpyCorps, SpyPortal, SpyScooter, kaput, blammo, satnav, invisibility shield, chihuahua
Heroes or Villains?	Phonetically regular compound and polysyllabic words	different, remembered, hero, heroine, villain, opinion, talent, championship, famous
	Prefixes/suffixes	**-ly** possibly, exactly, amazingly, badly, physically, mentally, especially, incredibly
	Context vocabulary	innocent, guilty, lawyer, judge, jury, verdict, media, journalist, evidence, beauty, beautiful

Air Scare

BY JAN BURCHETT AND SARA VOGLER

About this book

In this story, Tiger enters his model plane, *The Whizzer*, in a school flying contest, but Lucy goes all out to damage his and the other children's planes with some nasty tactics using her own model *Air Shark*. After Max shrinks to fix Tiger's plane, he takes over the controls and manages to outwit Lucy and win the competition for Tiger.

You will need

• *Spot the difference* Photocopy Master, *Teaching Handbook* for Year 3/P4

	Literacy Framework objective	**Target and assessment focus**
Speaking, listening, group interaction and drama	○ Explain process or present information, ensuring that items are clearly sequenced, relevant details are included and accounts are ended effectively 1.2	○ We can relate the events of the story and express events in a clear order **AF2**
Reading See also continuous reading objectives listed on page 9.	○ Infer characters' feelings in fiction 7.2 ○ Empathize with characters and debate moral dilemmas portrayed in texts 8.2	○ We can work out how characters might be feeling and give our reasons **AF3** ○ We can identify the moral dilemma in a story and talk about how we would feel if we were in a similar situation to a character **AF2/AF3**

The following notes provide a structure for three guided reading sessions. They are intended to be used flexibly; you may choose to focus on all three sessions or you could focus on one session and have the children read the rest of the book independently.

In Session 1, children will read Chapters 1 and 2. Children will then need to read Chapters 3 and 4 independently prior to Session 2. In Session 2, children will read Chapters 5 and 6. In Session 3, they will read Chapters 7 and 8.

Session I (Chapters I–2)

 Before reading

To activate prior knowledge and encourage prediction

- Ask the children if any of them have a remote-controlled vehicle. How do they work?
- Look at the cover of 'Air Scare' to identify that the story is about remote-controlled aeroplanes. Have any of the children seen one? Have they ever tried making a model aeroplane? Does the plane on the cover look as though it has been made or bought? (**activating prior knowledge, predicting**)

To support decoding and word recognition and introduce new vocabulary

- Study the vocabulary on pages 2–3.
- Draw children's attention to the /zz/ phoneme in *Whizzer*. Link this to *buzzing* (p.7). Now show them the word *prize* (p.4). Invite suggestions as to why there is only one 'z'.

To engage readers and support fluent reading

- Read pages 4 and 5. What do they think of Tiger's plane? Why do they think he called it the *Whizzer*? Can they relate the vocabulary in the text to the model? (**synthesizing**)
- Read to page 8. What do the children think of Lucy? Can they predict what will happen next? (**predicting**)

During reading

- Ask the children to read to the end of Chapter 2.
- As they read ask them to identify Max and Tiger's feelings about Lucy and possible reasons for Lucy's actions.
- If you have not already done so, ask the children what to do if they encounter a difficult word, modelling with an example from the book if necessary. Remind them of the more challenging vocabulary which you looked at before reading the book.

....>

 **After reading**

Returning to the text

- What do the children think about Lucy's behaviour? How do Max and Tiger feel about her? (**empathizing**)

....>

Building comprehension

- Ask children, in pairs, to look at the diagram of the *Air Shark* on pages 10–11 and talk about the similarities and differences between it and the *Whizzer*. What makes Tiger sure that it's not the same plane that Lucy made at school? Children could make notes on the *Spot the difference* Photocopy Master. (**inferring, deducing, drawing conclusions**)

Building fluency

- With you in role as Lucy, select volunteers to role play the characters of Tiger and Max and recreate Chapter 2 as an improvisation. The rest of the group then hot seat the characters about their feelings. (**empathizing, questioning**)

....>

- You may wish the children to make a note of how Tiger feels at various points of the story.

Building vocabulary

- Focus on the author's use of alternatives for the verb 'said', and adverbs and adverbial phrases. Use Post-it notes to cover up the words and invite children to suggest possibilities, saying the phrase aloud in the manner of their suggested word. Discuss how their word/s affect the reader's understanding of, and response to, the character.
- Before Session 2, ask the children to read Chapters 3 and 4 independently.

Session 2 (Chapters 5–6)

 Before reading

To activate prior knowledge and encourage prediction

- Discuss the development of the story in Chapters 3 and 4. (**summarizing**)
- Tiger seems more upset than ever. Why? What does Max do to help Tiger? (**recall**)
- Look at the picture on page 24 and the Chapter 5 heading. Can children predict what will happen? (**predicting**)

 During reading

- Ask the children to read Chapters 5 and 6.
- As they read ask them to focus on how the characters are feeling, especially at the end of each chapter.

 After reading

Returning to the text

- Ask the children to recap on what they have read. Ensure that they understand the convention, established in previous Project X stories, of the children's ability to shrink to micro size. (**summarizing**)

Building comprehension

- Look at page 25. How does Tiger feel? How would they feel in his position? (**determining importance, empathizing**)
- You may wish the children to start or continue plotting how Tiger feels at various points of the story.

Building fluency

- Explain to the children that a monologue is a dramatic technique to enable a character to reflect on a situation. In pairs, ask each child to take it in turn to talk through their feelings as Max or Tiger, with the other child eavesdropping. (**empathizing**)

· ➤

Assessment point

Can the children talk about the way they would feel if they were in a similar situation to a character? AF2/AF3

Session 3 (Chapters 7 and 8)

 Before reading

To activate prior knowledge and encourage prediction

- Review the story line up to the beginning of Chapter 7. Can children suggest what Lucy is planning to do next? (**activating prior knowledge, predicting**)

To support decoding and word recognition and introduce new vocabulary

- Practise decoding some of the phonically regular words in this book and listed in the vocabulary chart on page 10.

During reading

- Ask the children to read to the end of the story.
- As they read ask them to continue to focus on the feelings of the characters and how they change as the action progresses.
- If you have not already done so, ask the children what to do if they encounter a difficult word, modelling with an example from the book if necessary.

· ➤

Assessment point

Listen to individual children reading and make ongoing assessments on their decoding, sight vocabulary, approaches to tackling new words and their reading fluency. AF1

 After reading

Returning to the text

- What do the children think of each of the characters in the story? (**determining importance**)

Building comprehension

- Hot seat two volunteers as Max and Tiger while the rest of the group question them as reporters for the school or class newspaper on their success in the competition.

- As a group, you may wish the children to start, continue or complete noting how Tiger feels at various points of the story.

· ·>

Follow-up activities

Writing activities

- Write an account of the competition as if the children had been impartial spectators. (**longer writing task**)

- Using an appropriate ICT application, create tickets and a programme for the school's 'Grand Flying Competition' or for the air show that Max and Tiger will be going to. (**short writing task**)

Other literacy activities

- Improvise a scene between Mrs May and Lucy after the competition in which Lucy has to explain her actions. (**speaking and listening**)

- Pretend to be a radio/TV broadcaster and create a commentary for the 'air fight' on pages 34–46. Use the pictures to structure the commentary. (**speaking and listening**)

Cross-curricular and thematic opportunities

- Talk about how tension is built up in the story by alternating long-shot with close-up illustrations of the aeroplanes. Invite the children to create their own graphic storyboard of an air fight or similar event using long-shots and close-ups. (**Art and design**)

- Find out about the first aeroplanes. (**History**)

- Make a range of paper aeroplanes to see which travel the furthest (and why). Investigate streamlining. Demonstrate drag and acceleration, upthrust and gravity. (**Science, DT**)

- Make model aeroplanes and include features such as ailerons, rudders and propellers. (**Art and design**)

- Use circle time to discuss the issues around cheating. (**PSHE**)

Heroine in Hiding

BY TONY BRADMAN

About this book

Dani Day, a junior scientist for NICE, has been deceptively led to working for Dr X in the NASTI department. He traps her inside the laboratory, wanting her to work night and day to fix the watches which are vital components of his X-machine. Dani shrinks herself to escape and hijacks an X-Pod to track down the children to stop them using the watches. She succeeds but the children manage to convince her that they can help her on her mission to stop Dr X.

You will need

- *Top secret invention* Photocopy Master, *Teaching Handbook* for Year 3/P4

	Literacy Framework objective	Target and assessment focus
Speaking, listening, group interaction and drama	○ Sustain conversation, explain or give reasons for their views or choices 1.3	○ We can take part in a discussion and respond to questions, giving reasons for our answers **AF3**
Reading See also continuous reading objectives listed on page 9.	○ Infer characters' feelings in fiction 7.2 ○ Use syntax, context and word structure to build their store of vocabulary as they read for meaning 7.4	○ We can work out how characters might be feeling and give our reasons **AF2/3** ○ We can discuss the words the author has used **AF5**

The following notes provide a structure for three guided reading sessions. They are intended to be used flexibly; you may choose to focus on all three sessions or you could focus on one session and have the children read the rest of the book independently.

In Session 1, children will read Chapters 1 and 2. Children will then need to read Chapter 3 independently prior to Session 2. In Session 2, children will read Chapters 4 and 5. In Session 3, children will read Chapters 6 and 7.

Session 1 (Chapters 1–2)

 Before reading

To activate prior knowledge and encourage prediction

○ Ask the children to think back to previous books they have read in the Project X series involving the watches which allow the children wearing them to shrink. Share thoughts and recollections about their usefulness in different situations. Pose questions as to where they might come from. (**activating prior knowledge, predicting**)

To preview the text

○ Look at the cover and title page of the book. Ask children for comments on the woman's appearance. What can they infer about Dani from the artist's portrayal of her? What is the silver box?

○ Read through the fact file about Dani on page 2. Go through the items to ensure basic understanding of nano technology and the advanced level subjects. What can the children infer about Dani from her fact file? (**previewing**)

To support decoding and word recognition and introduce new vocabulary

○ Write up NICE on the board. What does it mean? Can the children think of other acronyms? NASTI is used later in the story. Can children think of what it could stand for? (Allow them to find out the answer later when they read the answer in the story.) Can they infer anything from the acronyms about these places? (**deducing, inferring, drawing conclusions**)

To engage readers and support fluent reading

- Read page 4. How has Dr X used his knowledge of Dani to persuade her to work for him? (**determining importance**)

- Continue reading to the end of Chapter 1. Refer to the illustrations: how has Dr X changed? Can they find the sentence which supports the artist's portrayal of him? (**deducing, inferring**)

- How might Dani be feeling at the end of the chapter? Encourage children to give reasons for their answers. (**empathizing**)

 During reading

- Ask the children to read Chapter 2.
- As they read ask them to focus on Dani's changing emotions.

 After reading

Building fluency

- Discuss the use of scientific vocabulary. You could create flash cards of the key words (see context vocabulary in chart on page 10) and keep them in a silver box. Use them for games, e.g. children pretend to be scientists and are given the words if they can spell or define them.

- Before Session 2, ask the children to read Chapter 3 independently.

· >

Assessment point

Can the children talk about the writer's use of scientific words? AF5

Before reading

- Invite children to summarize the events in Chapter 3. What has Dr X created to track down the children? (**summarizing**, **recall**)
- What do the children think Dani might do? (**predicting**)

 During reading

- Ask children to read Chapters 4 and 5.
- As they read ask them to focus on what Dani's response is to the situation.
- If you have not already done so, ask the children what to do if they encounter a difficult word, modelling with an example from the book if necessary. Remind them of the more challenging vocabulary which you looked at before reading the book.

> **Assessment point**
>
> Listen to individual children reading and make ongoing assessments on their decoding, sight vocabulary, approaches to tackling new words and their reading fluency. **AF1**

 After reading

Returning to the text

- Briefly review what the children have read. What do they think of Dani's response? Is she a heroine? Is Dr X a villain? How would they describe the characters and roles of Plug and Socket? Have they recognised Cat, Ant, Tiger and Max and made links with previous stories? (**deducing**, **inferring**, **drawing conclusions**)

Building comprehension

- Divide the group into two and ask one group to draw a diagram of an X-bot and the other group to draw an X-pod. In role as expert scientists ask each group to present information about their invention to the other group. (**determining importance**)
- Ask each group to think of questions to ask the other group about the invention. (**questioning**)

> **Assessment point**
>
> Can children take part in a discussion and respond to questions, giving reasons for their answers? **AF3**

Before reading

To activate prior knowledge and encourage prediction

- Review the situation at the end of the previous session. Can the children suggest what will happen next? (**predicting**)

 During reading

- Ask the children to read Chapters 6 and 7.
- As they read ask them to continue to notice how Dani is feeling.

 After reading

Returning to the text

- How did Dani find the children? What did the children think when they saw her? (**inferring**, **deducing**)

Building comprehension

- What do the children think about the character of Dani? What do they think she will do when she gets back to NASTI? (**determining importance**, **predicting**)

· ·>

Assessment point

Are the children able to show understanding of a main character, her changing emotions and reasons for her behaviour? AF2/3

Follow-up activities

Writing activities

- Write a further chapter for this book or the opening chapter for the next book. (**longer writing task**)
- With a partner, write and illustrate a catalogue of Dr X's inventions. (**longer writing task**)
- Create a fact file like Dani's for other characters in the story. (**short writing task**)

Other literacy activities

- Dramatize scenes from the story, filming them, if possible. (**speaking and listening**)

Cross-curricular and thematic opportunities

- Make shoe box models of NICE and NASTI. Use them to create an animation of the story using small world people. (**DT**)
- Investigate appropriate sound effects and music to use in the dramatized scenes (see Other literacy activities). (**Music**)
- Draw and annotate further inventions for Dr X using the *Top secret invention* Photocopy Master. (**Art and design**)
- Use circle time to discuss children's ideas about what would make the world a better place. Alternatively, discuss what would make their parents or carers proud of them. (**PSHE**)

Dr X's Top IO Villains

BY ANDREA SMITH

About this book

This non-fiction text highlights those characters from books and films that Dr X considers to be his all-time best villains.

You will need

- *Dr X's Top 10 Villains summary* Photocopy Master, *Teaching Handbook* for Year 3/P4
- *Villain profile* Photocopy Master, *Teaching Handbook* for Year 3/P4

	Literacy Framework objective	**Target and assessment focus**
Speaking, listening, group interaction and drama	○ Sustain conversation, explain or give reasons for their views or choices **I.3**	○ We can talk about our views and give reasons for our choices **AF2**
Reading See also continuous reading objectives listed on page 9.	○ Identify how different texts are organized **7.3** ○ Share and compare reasons for reading preferences extending the range of books read **8.I**	○ We know some of the ways that reference texts organize their information **AF4** ○ We can talk about the effect of different texts on the reader **AF6**

The following notes provide a structure for three guided reading sessions. They are intended to be used flexibly; you may choose to focus on all three sessions or you could focus on one session and have the children read the rest of the book independently. In Session 1, children will read to the end of page 8. In Session 2, children will select sections to read from pages 9–29. In Session 3 children will focus on pages 9–32 along with the whole text, which the children will revisit during the session.

Session I (pages 2–8)

 Before reading

To activate prior knowledge and encourage prediction

- Look at the front cover: Do the children know what a villain is? Who is Dr X? (**activating prior knowledge**)
- Who would the children include in their list of top villains from books, comics and films? Make a note of them.

To preview the text

- Skim through the book to find out which villains Dr X has chosen and compare these with the children's choices. Do the children have any in common? Are there some they haven't come across? (**previewing**)

To engage readers and support fluent reading

- Look at the section on Darth Vader together. Draw children's attention to the different ways that the information has been presented.
- Read the 'biography' of Darth Vader on page 4 to the children. Talk about the features of style used by the author of a biography.
- In pairs, ask the children to read page 5.
- Talk about what they have found out about Darth Vader.

During reading

- Ask the children to read up to the end of page 8.
- As they read ask them to look at the ways the information has been presented.
- If you have not already done so, ask them what to do if they encounter a difficult word, modelling with an example from the book if necessary. Remind them of the more challenging vocabulary which you looked at before reading the book.

....>

 After reading

Returning to the text

- Ask the children to find two things which the villains on pages 3–8 have in common and two differences. (**deducing**, **summarizing**)

Building comprehension

- Which of the two villains seems to them to be the most evil? Can they find reasons from the text to support their argument? (**deducing**, **inferring**, **drawing conclusions**)
- Invite comments about the bad-o-meter. Can they suggest ratings for some of their own villains, with reasons? (**synthesizing**)

Building fluency

- Divide the children into two groups, each focusing on one of the two villains. Allow a few minutes for them to reread the text and come up with a comment about the way in which information is provided. They can use sticky notes to record their ideas.

....>

Assessment point
Listen to individual children reading and make ongoing assessments on their decoding, sight vocabulary, approaches to tackling new words and their reading fluency. AF1

Assessment point
Can the children recognize the different ways that information is presented in an information text? AF4

Session 2 (pages 9–29)

 Before reading

To preview the text

- Walk the children through the book again and briefly comment on the villains who are profiled.

To support decoding and word recognition and introduce new vocabulary

- Clarify any unfamiliar technical language such as *robotics, chemistry, cloning, biology* (p.13) and *toxin* (p.22) and colloquial phrases such as *nuff said* (p.25).

 During reading

- Talk about choices in reading, being able to hold a conversation about what has been read and giving reasons for opinions.
- Ask the children to select which villains they would like to read about, making their own choices of four to five from the ones remaining.
- As they read ask them to take note of the information which describes the unpleasant characteristics of each villain.
- If you have not already done so, ask them what to do if they encounter a difficult word, modelling with an example from the book if necessary. Remind them of the more challenging vocabulary which you looked at before reading the book.

 After reading

Returning to the text

- Ask the children to tell a partner which villains they chose to read about and what they learnt about the villains.

Building comprehension

- Hold a debate to decide which villain is the most unpleasant. Encourage the children to use the information in the text to support their ideas and point out the use of powerful vocabulary when trying to persuade or defend an argument. They could use the *Dr X's Top 10 Villains summary* Photocopy Master to help them present their arguments. (**deducing, inferring, drawing conclusions**)
- Alternatively, debate the scariness of one of Dr X's villains compared to a villain from other books, films or comics.

> **Assessment point**
>
> Can they say which texts were most successful in creating the intended effect on the reader? AF6

Building fluency

- In pairs, ask the children to choose a villain and use the information in the text to present as a radio broadcast. They should decide who will read which sections, what tone and expression to adopt and whether to include sound effects. (**determining importance, visualizing and other sensory responses**)

Session 3 (pages 9–32)

 Before reading

To activate prior knowledge and encourage prediction

- Review the text by asking children to share their discoveries and ideas on the villains they have read about. (**activating prior knowledge**)

To support decoding and word recognition and introduce new vocabulary

- You may wish to point out some of the high or medium frequency words or practise decoding some of the phonically regular words in this book and listed in the vocabulary chart on page 11.

 During reading

- Invite the children to choose a villain which they have not yet discussed.
- As they read ask them to think about the details of the villain which make them interesting.
- If you have not already done so, ask them what to do if they encounter a difficult word, modelling with an example from the book if necessary. Remind them of the more challenging vocabulary which you looked at before reading the book.

 After reading

Returning to the text

- Ask the children which villains they found most and least interesting. How did the way the information was presented influence their thinking? Which one would they like to find out more about? (**personal response**)

Assessment point
Can the children sustain a conversation and give reasons to support their choices and ideas? AF2

Building comprehension

- Why are villains important in stories? (**synthesizing**)
- Invite the children to choose one of the villains which they have found particularly interesting. Tell them that they are going to become an expert on that villain and ask them to come up with a number of questions based on the text which an expert would be able to answer. (**questioning**, **determining importance**)
- Use the questions generated by the children to stage a Mastermind-type competition. You may want to give children the opportunity to extend their interest through further research.

Follow-up activities

Writing activities

- Encourage children to invent a villain for a story or comic strip by using the *Villain profile* Photocopy Master. (**short writing task**)
- Children could research a villain from a story, comic or film of their choice for a mini project. (**longer writing task**)

Other literacy activities

- Create a display featuring a range of villains, perhaps incorporating a rogues' gallery (as on page 2). Provide opportunities for expressing preferences.

Cross-curricular and thematic opportunities

- Find out about some villains from history. Include biographies of them in the book corner. (**History**)
- In circle time, discuss issues around good and bad people. Who do the children recognize as good and bad role models in fiction and/or in real life? What distinctions do they draw between real life and fantasy? (**PSHE**)
- There are many sophisticated scientific ideas behind some of the villains and their domains in this text. Children may want further clarification about genetic modification, mutation, implants, cloning, robotics. (**Science**)
- Draw or paint pictures of villains for the book corner display. Make a bad-o-meter (and perhaps a good-o-meter for heroes!) (**Art**)

Jake Jones v Vlad the Bad

BY JOANNA NADIN

About this book

Jake Jones, SpyCorps' special agent, is on a mission to save items beginning with 'v' being stolen by the evil Vlad the Bad. Using his powers of deduction, and with help from his spy gadgets, he discovers that the next and final 'v' word to be taken by Vlad the Bad is Violet – Jake's sister. Jake saves his sister from becoming a dog-treat for Vlad's chihuahua!

You will need

- *Code breakers* Photocopy Master, *Teaching Handbook* for Year 3/P4

	Literacy Framework objective	Target and assessment focus
Speaking, listening, group interaction and drama	○ Develop and use specific vocabulary in different contexts 1.4	○ We can choose and use words to fit the context **AF2**
Reading See also continuous reading objectives listed on page 9.	○ Use syntax, context and word structure to build their store of vocabulary as they read for meaning **7.4** ○ Explore how different texts appeal to readers using varied sentence structures and descriptive language **7.5**	○ We can make sense of and use words collected from our reading **AF1/2** ○ We can identify effective sentences and descriptive language in our reading **AF5**

The following notes provide a structure for three guided reading sessions. They are intended to be used flexibly; you may choose to focus on all three sessions or you could focus on one session and have the children read the rest of the book independently.

In Session 1, children will read Chapters 1 and 2. Children will then need to read Chapter 3 independently, prior to Session 2. In Session 2, children will read Chapter 4. Children will then need to read Chapter 5 independently, prior to Session 3. In Session 3, children will read Chapters 6 and 7.

Session I (Chapters I–2)

 Before reading

To activate prior knowledge and encourage prediction

- Look at the title of the book. What can the children infer from it about the characters and the possible plot? (**activating prior knowledge, predicting, inferring**)

To preview the text

- Read the fact file on page 2 together. What sort of boy is Jake?
- Ask children, in pairs, to read the fact file on Vlad the Bad. What sort of character is he? Do the children recognize these stereotypes? (**inferring, deducing, drawing conclusions**)

To support decoding and word recognition and introduce new vocabulary

- Make simple books with the children to use as Spy Word notebooks. Children can create a cover using the SpyCorps logo with their own name substituted. Encourage children to collect words during their reading.
- Read pages 4 and 5 and model how to identify spy vocabulary, such as *transmitter* and *HQ*. Encourage an investigative interest in the words.
- You may also wish to point out some of the high or medium frequency words or practise decoding some of the phonically regular words in this book and listed in the vocabulary chart on page 11.

To engage readers and support fluent reading

- Review pages 4 and 5 for meaning. Why has Jake got to deal with Violet?

During reading

- Ask the children to read Chapter 2.
- As they read ask them to think about what Jake's mission might be.
- Ask the children what to do if they encounter a difficult word, modelling with an example from the book if necessary. Remind them of the more challenging vocabulary which you looked at before reading the book.
- Fast finishers can start identifying vocabulary for their Spy Word notebook.

· ·>

 After reading

Returning to the text

- Ask children to tell a partner what they think Jake's mission might be and why. (**inferring**, **deducing**)

Building comprehension

- Why does Jake detest Vince Van Spangle? (**deducing**, **drawing conclusions**)
- What do the children think has happened to him? (**predicting**)

Building vocabulary

- Collect a list of words beginning with 'v' which are mentioned in the text. Discuss, record and save them on an interactive whiteboard for Session 2.
- Before Session 2, ask the children to read Chapter 3 independently.

> **Assessment point**
>
> Listen to individual children reading and make ongoing assessments on their decoding, sight vocabulary, approaches to tackling new words and their reading fluency. AF1

Session 2 (Chapter 4)

 Before reading

To activate prior knowledge and encourage prediction

- Ask the children to tell a partner what has happened in the story so far. (**summarizing**)
- What were some of the 'v' items that Jake thought Vlad might have stolen? (**recall**)

To support decoding and word recognition and introduce new vocabulary

- Point out some of the high frequency words or practise decoding some phonically regular words listed in the vocabulary chart on page 11.

During reading

- Ask the children to read Chapter 4.
- As they read ask them to focus on the key points of the plot.

Assessment point

Listen to individual children reading and make ongoing assessments on their decoding, sight vocabulary, approaches to tackling new words and their reading fluency. AF1

After reading

Returning to the text

- Take it in turns round the group to contribute a sentence which details the key points of the story. (**summarizing**)

Building fluency

- Go back to pages 13, 14 and 15 to explore the vowels that have been removed from the words. Can they still make meaning of the words? Encourage them to be curious about word structure through visualizing other words in which vowels have been removed.
- Ask the children to reread from 'And if verbs disappeared ...' on page 14 to the end of page 15. Why do they think the writer used the ellipses? Short sentences? Question marks? (**deducing**, **inferring**, **drawing conclusions**)

Assessment point

Can the children identify the writer's intention in using these structures and features? AF5

Building vocabulary

- Add the new 'v' words to the list you saved on the interactive whiteboard. Check that the children understand what they are and that they are nouns. Can they think of more 'v' words to add? Investigate arranging the words in alphabetical order.
- What vocabulary have they identified for their Spy Word notebooks? Discuss the compound words – *SpyPortal* and *SpyScooter*. Invite comments about why the words are run together with a capital for the second part of the compound word.

- Can they invent some more words following the same pattern?

··>

- Before Session 3, ask the children to read Chapter 5 independently.

Session 3 (Chapters 6–7)

 Before reading

To activate prior knowledge and encourage prediction

- Recap the story up to the end of Chapter 5 by creating a story map on a sheet of paper. Starting with Jake's watch beeping while eating his breakfast, let the children determine what should be included as the main points of the story. (**recall, determining importance**)

To support decoding and word recognition and introduce new vocabulary

- You may also wish to point out some of the high or medium frequency words or practise decoding some of the phonically regular words in this book and listed in the vocabulary chart on page 11.

 During reading

- Ask the children to Chapters 6 and 7.
- As they read ask them to focus on key points to include on the story map.

··>

 After reading

Returning to the text

- Complete the rest of the story map collaboratively, determining which points are vital to the map and which could be left out. (**recall, determining importance**)

Building comprehension

- Ask the children to identify how the author has used words and sentences effectively. Give each child a different page to focus on; allow them a few minutes to find the word, the phrase and the sentence that they like best, sharing these with the group.

• >

Assessment point

Can the children identify and comment on the sentences and language choices that they found effective? **AF5**

Building fluency

- In pairs, ask children to role play the telephone conversation in which Jake contacts Harry Handsome at HQ to tell him what has happened. (**synthesizing**)

• >

Assessment point

Do the children choose and use words from the text, to fit the context? **AF2**

Follow-up activities

Writing activities

- Ask each child to create their own secret agent fact file. They also could invent and create a fact file for an enemy. (**short writing task**)
- Write a story in which the child is the hero. (**longer writing task**)
- Write a version of the story as a play to perform with puppets. (**longer writing task**)

Other literacy activities

- Show children how to use the 'Find and replace' function in Word on the computer and then, in pairs, write secret messages to each other in which vowels or other letters have been changed or removed.
- Children could crack the code on the *Code breakers* Photocopy Master.

Cross-curricular and thematic opportunities

- Invent a special weapon. Use a computer to draw it and write a description of what it can do. Then make it using junk materials. (**DT**)
- Make puppets to use when performing the play script (see Writing activities). (**Art and design**)
- Draw a picture which contains only things that begin with the same letter. (**Art and design**)

Heroes or Villains?

BY HAYDN MIDDLETON

About this book

This non-fiction text looks at how there are two sides to people – good and bad. It gives facts about the behaviour of famous sportsmen, a businessman and an artist – both their virtuous and morally dubious practices. These discussions then leave readers to come to their own verdict of them.

You will need

• *Hero or Villain?* Photocopy Master, *Teaching Handbook* for Year 3/P4

	Literacy Framework objective	Target and assessment focus
Speaking, listening, group interaction and drama	○ Follow up others' points and show whether they agree or disagree in whole-class discussion 2.1	○ We can back up our ideas in a discussion with evidence from a text **AF2**
Reading See also continuous reading objectives listed on page 9.	○ Empathize with characters and debate moral dilemmas portrayed in texts 8.2 ○ Identify features that writers use to provoke readers' reactions 8.3	○ We can look at both sides of an argument and see the issue from more than one point of view **AF3** ○ We can understand that the way authors present information sometimes shows us how they feel about a subject **AF6**

The following notes provide a structure for three guided reading sessions. They are intended to be used flexibly; you may choose to focus on all three sessions or you could focus on one session and have the children read the rest of the book independently.

In Session 1, children will read up to page 15. Children will then need to read pages 16–23 independently prior to Session 2. In Session 2, children will read pages 24–27. In Session 3, they will read pages 28–30.

Session 1 (pages 2–15)

 Before reading

To activate prior knowledge and encourage prediction

- As a group, discuss the differences between a hero and a villain. Ask them to predict who might be featured in the book. (**activating prior knowledge**, **predicting**)

To preview the text

- Look at the contents page. What information can the children deduce about the book from this? (**deducing**)

To support decoding and word recognition and introduce new vocabulary

- Do the children understand the terms *innocent* and *guilty*? Can they give a definition and an example of each?
- Explain to the children that the definitions of words written in bold can be found in the glossary on page 31. In pairs, ask them to look up the definitions of *innocent* and *guilty* in the glossary.

To engage readers and support fluent reading

- Look at the heading on page 4. Can the children explain what it means in a broader context?
- Ask them to read to the end of page 5. Review the newspaper headlines in light of the questions at the bottom of the page.

During reading

- Ask the children to read to the end of page 15. Point out that they are going to read about two ways of seeing a person.

- If you have not already done so, ask the children what to do if they encounter a difficult word, modelling with an example from the book if necessary. Remind them of the more challenging vocabulary which you looked at before reading the book.

· >

 After reading

Returning to the text

- Reread the text on Zidane and ask which members of the group think he is a hero, giving reasons through reference to the text. Repeat with those who think he is a villain. (**inferring**, **deducing**, **drawing conclusions**)

Building comprehension

- Explain that you want the children to reflect on the two text presentations: which was most persuasive? Can we believe what we read? (**adopting a critical stance**)

- How does the comment by one of Zidane's teammates (on page 9) influence the reader? (**determining importance**)

Building fluency

- Divide the group into two, with one group taking on the role of 'Good guy Gates' and the other 'Bad guy Bill'. Give them a few minutes to discuss their side of the story, then hot seat each group with the others asking them questions. (**questioning**)

· >

Building vocabulary

- Zidane is referred to as a 'beautiful' player. He is also referred to as a beast. Can the children make the literary connection?

- Before Session 2, ask the children to read pages 16–23 independently.

Session 2 (pages 24–27)

 Before reading

To activate prior knowledge and encourage prediction

- Ask the children to describe the 'two sides of the story' for each person featured on pages 16–23. Do they agree with the author's viewpoint? Why or why not? (**deducing, inferring, drawing conclusions**)

· ·>

 During reading

- Ask the children to read pages 24–27.
- As they read, ask them to consider how and why the author presents the reader with more than one opinion.

 After reading

Returning to the text

- Ask the children, in pairs, to list words and phrases that endorse a featured person from the book as a hero and a 'villain' on the *Hero or villain?* Photocopy Master.

Building comprehension

- Ask the children to look at the section on Schumacher and think of a comment they would like to say to him. Then ask them to stand in a circle with a volunteer in role as Schumacher standing in the middle. Children take it in turns to say their comment, after which 'Schumacher' responds to what was said. (**determining importance**)

Session 3 (pages 28–30)

 Before reading

- Review the overall theme of the text with the children.

During reading

- Ask the children to read pages 28–30.

 After reading

Returning to the text

- What do the children think of the people they have read about in this book?

....>

Building comprehension

- Why should people be wary of believing everything they read or hear? How could this apply to the children?

Follow-up activities

Writing activities

- Read traditional tales in which the bad character (e.g. the big bad wolf) has been portrayed as 'the goody' – and vice versa – and write a story based on a role reversal. (**longer writing task**)
- In pairs, make a 'guilty and innocent' poster of a real or fictional character. This could be done using ICT. (**short writing task**)

Other literacy activities

- In a small group, role play a court scene in which the cases for being innocent or guilty are presented for a character from fiction, e.g. Goldilocks. Make a video recording to share with an audience. (**speaking and listening**)

Cross-curricular and thematic opportunities

- Hold a debate or mock trial to present two sides of a story relating to a character from a history study. (**History**)
- Use circle time to discuss the moral issues of believing everything you hear, distorting the truth and being fair. (**PSHE**)
- Make reference to fair testing. (**Science**)
- Keeping a balance – investigate weighing using pan scales and link this with the icon for Justice. (**Maths**)